DAILY MEDITATIONS FOR CHILDREN

Jesus, engrave it on my heart,
That Thou the one thing needful art;
I could from all things parted be,
But never, never, Lord, from Thee.

DAILY MEDITATIONS
FOR CHILDREN

By MRS. G. W. HINSDALE

STRAHAN AND CO., PUBLISHERS

56, LUDGATE HILL, LONDON

1868

This Book is designed to be a companion to 'Daily Devotions for Children.' I anticipate the feeling which many parents may have that children cannot be expected to *meditate* on Sacred Truth. Of course they will not, unless they are taught to do so. But will not a child's mind grow and work in the way in which it is led? Do we all give children the credit which they deserve, for thoughtfulness and spiritual perception?

The power of reflection, though weak in the beginning, will increase by use, and to learn to appropriate God's blessed Word to ourselves is an infinite gain. Though these meditations fall so far short of what they ought to be, in view of my object, still I hope that many children will find pleasure and profit in reading them more than once.

I have gathered thoughts and suggestions, which it seemed to me might be useful; and I have tried to write out the natural ideas of a thoughtful child after reading its daily portion of the Divine Word. May it please the good Shepherd, by this humble book, to show his lambs the heavenly pastures where he feeds his flock!

G. W. II.

DEAR CHILDREN,—*After reading God's Holy Word, did you ever leave the book open before you, and talk aloud to yourself about its precious truth? Did you ever think that the Bible is God's message of love to you? Try to think of what you read, and "hide God's Word in your heart, that you may love Him, and that you may not sin against Him." Ask the Holy Spirit " to take of the things of Christ and to show them unto you."*

G. W. H.

DAILY MEDITATIONS.

FIRST DAY.

For God so loved the world that he gave his only begotten Son, that whosoever believeth in him should not perish, but have everlasting life. John iii. 16.

He will save, he will watch over thee with joy. Zeph. iii. 17.

And he arose, and came to his father. But when he was yet a great way off, his father saw him, and had compassion, and ran, and fell on his neck, and kissed him. Luke xv. 20.

I LIKE to sit and imagine how the father of the poor prodigal looked when he saw his son afar off. I think I can see him reaching out his kind arms as he ran to meet him. He had not a thought of turning the poor young man away, though he knew all about his foolish and wicked conduct. He could hardly bear to hear him confess his wrong-doing, or wait to give him an opportunity to ask forgiveness. No; he was the poor prodigal's kind and patient father, and he felt in haste to bring him into the house, and to put on him garments such as his son should wear, and to put a ring upon his finger, and to rejoice over him with singing!

It is a beautiful story. I read it over and over again, and it seems to tell me of God's great and wonderful love to us sinners who have wandered away from him. It makes me think of the many times my parents and friends have forgiven my disobedience and unkindness and ingratitude. I remember how tenderly they have treated me, and how they have taken me in their arms and drawn me close to them when they felt sure of my sorrow for my faults.

I'm sure that the Saviour means to invite us to return to God from all our wicked ways. How can I be afraid or unwilling to

FOR CHILDREN.

9

tell my heavenly Father all about my sins? He does not bid us come to him that he may censure and condemn us. Jesus, the Redeemer, says that he did not come into the world to condemn us, but to save us. Oh, let me never be afraid to go and tell Jesus all the sins of my wicked life! I will not think of God as an angry judge—though I know that he will call me to give an account of my conduct at the solemn judgment day. I will remember how he sent his dear Son to die for sinners. I will remember this story of the penitent prodigal, in which God represents himself as a loving father rejoicing to take back into his arms his unhappy and penitent son.

God, the holy Father, sent his beloved Son into the world because he longed to have us return unto him, that he might save and bless us.

Not a word of stern upbraiding,
  Grieved his sad and suffering soul,
When the boy his sin confessing
  To his father's bosom stole!

DAILY MEDITATIONS

Both were glad, yet both were weeping,
   While they stood with arms entwined;
And that young heart's anxious beating,
   Proved the grief that filled his mind.

Songs of joy were echoed sweetly,
   Through the halls of that dear home;
And the father's love told quickly,
   That the wanderer had come.

Overcome with grief and weeping,
   Lying on his father's breast,
The poor boy his sins confessing,
   Sank at last to peace and rest.

FOR CHILDREN.

SECOND DAY.

How beautiful upon the mountains are the feet of him that bringeth good tidings, that publisheth peace ; that bringeth good tidings of good, that publisheth salvation.   Isaiah lii. 7.

And the angel said unto them, Fear not ; for, behold, I bring you good tidings of great joy. which shall be to all people.   Luke ii. 10.

The gospel of the grace of God.   Acts xx. 24.

The gospel of Christ.   Rom. i. 16.

The gospel of your salvation.   Eph. i. 13.

Jesus came into Galilee, preaching the gospel of the kingdom of God,

And saying, The time is fulfilled, and the kingdom of God is at hand : repent ye, and believe the gospel.   Mark i. 14–15.

THE word Gospel means good news or glad tidings. It is in the precious Gospel that we read of the grace and mercy of God to our sinful souls.

The books which were written by Matthew, Mark, Luke, and John, contain the history of Jesus, so that we are told the story of his life by four different men who knew and loved him. They wrote out God's message of love to sinners as they heard it from Jesus' lips; and they explained to us how the holy life of the dear Saviour obtained precious rewards and blessings for us, and how his death upon the cross procured the pardon of our sins. I think they did well to call their books "the Gospel," for certainly no such good news had ever been sent to the world before. It was, indeed, glad tidings to all who heard or read of the Saviour's love! It was the gospel of our salvation, brought to us from God by Christ the Redeemer! He came saying, "Repent ye, and believe the Gospel." He told us that if we were sorry for our sins we might believe the good news of God's willingness to forgive us; and to all the poor and wretched around him he preached the precious Gospel. He told us that he came to take our place, and to suffer the

FOR CHILDREN.

13

punishment which the holy law required for our sins; and that his own holy life and perfect obedience should merit for us a place in heaven. Oh, what a Saviour Jesus is! He has obtained eternal happiness for all who love him; he has promised to prepare us by his Holy Spirit to live with him in heaven. He tells us that God will mercifully receive us when we die if we have truly repented of our sins, and tried to live a holy life.

O God, please to make my heart pure from sin in the blood of Jesus, and help me to rejoice in the glad tidings which tell us of all the good things which thou art so willing to give us for the sake of what thy dear Son has done and suffered for us! Amen.

DAILY MEDITATIONS

14

THIRD DAY.

This is my beloved son, in whom I am well pleased. Matt. iii. 17.

The Lord is well pleased for his righteousness sake. Is. xlii. 21.

Be ye holy. Lev. xx. 7.

Walk before me, and be thou perfect. Gen. xvii. 1.

But we are all as an unclean thing, and all our righteousnesses are as filthy rags. Is. lxiv. 6.

He hath made us accepted in the Beloved. Eph. i. 6.

IT makes me very happy when I see that my conduct pleases my parents, and that they are satisfied with my work when they have given me a particular thing to do. I feel as if nothing could induce me to neglect their wishes, when to gain their approval is so sweet. But oh, it grieves me to think that God is so dissatisfied with me! I should like to please him perfectly, so that

FOR CHILDREN. 15

he would not be disappointed in me! I should like to do always just those things he commands and wishes me to do; just those things which he expects me to do! I wish that there were never in my heart any feelings but just those a little Christian should have! In one of David's Psalms it says: "The Lord looked down from heaven upon the children of men" to see if there were any that were good, and there was "not one." And yet it does not comfort me that I am like everybody else in the world; I think it makes me wish all the more that I could please God, and win his smile, to make me happy. At any rate I will try to obey his commands; I will try to watch my heart and keep it pure.

How thankful I am to know that I am not going *alone* before God to stand clothed in my own righteousness. Indeed, I need not present myself to God at all for his *approval*—I must not do that. Jesus "appears in the presence of God for us," and God says of him: "This is my beloved Son,

DAILY MEDITATIONS

in whom I am *well pleased.*" The Saviour came into the world to take my place, and to bear my punishment—to suffer and die for me. And he *lived* for me too, he obeyed the law for me, so that I might have his righteousness as a beautiful robe to cover my sin-stained soul. God is well pleased *even with me* for his righteousness' sake. If I am penitent for my sins, God will not look at them; he will not mention them to me any more; but he will look upon Jesus, in whom he is always well pleased, and who offers himself to God in my place.

This comforts me more than I can tell; but still I want to be holy *myself!* What infinite mercy it is in God to accept me through Jesus in this way! Certainly he expects that I will try to please him in my own life! Oh, my dear heavenly Father, give me thy holy Spirit to help me; do not let me be willing to offend thee, who art so good and merciful to me! My disobedience to my parents would disappoint and grieve their hearts. O God, thou hast done infi-

FOR CHILDREN.

17

nitely more for me than my earthly parents
can ever do; let me not be a disobedient
and rebellious child to thee! Amen.

Jesus! thy robe ot righteousness
My beauty is,—my glorious dress:
'Mid flaming worlds, in this arrayed,
With joy shall I lift up my head.

When from the dust of death, I rise
To claim my mansion in the skies,
Ev'n then shall this be all my plea,—
" Jesus hath lived and died for me."

B

18 *DAILY MEDITATIONS*

FOURTH DAY.

Search the Scriptures. John v. 9.

And that from a child thou hast known the Holy Scriptures which are able to make thee wise unto salvation through faith, which is in Christ Jesus.

All Scripture is given by inspiration of God. 2 Tim. iii. 15, 16.

Thy word have I hid in mine heart, that I might not sin against thee. Ps. cxix. 11.

Thy word is a lamp unto my feet, and a light unto my path. Ps. cxix. 105.

WHAT a wonderful book the Bible is! My simple and ignorant thoughts are all confused when I try to think of the ages since its first chapters were written. How many little children have learned to repeat the beautiful parables and the sweet Psalms of David! How many poor, lonely prisoners, and sick and suffering people, have comforted themselves with the precious promises in the

FOR CHILDREN. 19

Bible! How sweet the words of Jesus have been to all those who have loved him!

This Holy Book is able to make us wise unto salvation, for it shows us the path of life, and leads us to the precious Saviour, who is able and willing to save us. No captain, though he were ever so wise, would go to sea without his compass; and I know that I shall never guide myself aright if I neglect to inquire which way God's wisdom and will direct me. I will study my Bible more than any other book. Why should I take such pains to study the books containing earthly knowledge, and give so much less attention to this gracious and holy Book?

I should like to know what will become of our Bibles when this world is all passed away. Shall we never have them again? It seems to me that it would be a great pleasure lost—or left behind. But God knows best what we shall need or enjoy in another world. One thing I will do; I will be sure, if possible, to know all that is written in the precious Bible before I die. I know that I

DAILY MEDITATIONS

can understand but a small portion of it; but, certainly, I will try to read and remember as much as I can of God's Holy Word. Blessed Spirit, help me to believe and to love my precious Bible!

"The Bible is my chart,
By it the seas I know;
I cannot with it part—
It rocks and sands doth show.
It is my chart and compass too,
Whose needle points for ever true."

FOR CHILDREN.

21

FIFTH DAY.

Thou knowest not what a day may bring forth. Prov. xxvii. 1.

And I saw in the right hand of him that sat on the throne a book written within and on the back side, sealed with seven seals.

And I saw a strong angel proclaiming with a loud voice, Who is worthy to open the book, and to loose the seals thereof?

And no man in heaven, nor in earth, neither under the earth, was able to open the book, neither to look thereon.

And I wept much, because there was no man found worthy to open and to read the book, neither to look thereon.

And one of the elders saith unto me, Weep not : behold, the Lion of the tribe of Juda, the Root of David, hath prevailed to open the book, and to loose the seven seals thereof.

And I beheld, and lo, in the midst of the throne and of the four beasts, and in the midst of the elders, stood a Lamb as it had been slain,

DAILY MEDITATIONS

having seven horns and seven eyes, which are the seven spirits of God sent forth into all the earth.

And he came and took the book out of the right hand of him that sat upon the throne. Rev. v. 1–7.

I OFTEN wish that I knew how and where my life will be spent, and what God will permit to happen to me. I think, with tears in my eyes, of the time when I shall be left alone without my dear parents—for certainly I should feel alone if they were gone, though I had ever so many other friends. When I see poor invalids confined with pain and weakness to their beds for years, I think to myself—perhaps my heavenly Father will find that I need such suffering to make me obedient and humble, as he wishes me to be. But there is no use of my thinking of all these things. No one can read the book of the future, and know or even guess what will come to pass. It is a sealed book, and we need not be surprised at anything which happens. God knows everything which is before us in this world, and all the events of

FOR CHILDREN.

23

our life will be just as he intended they should be. He orders all things for us by his Son Jesus Christ, to whom he gave the book with the seven seals. No one could open the book but our dear Saviour, who is the Lamb of God slain for us. The winds and the sea obeyed him when he was upon the earth, and all power in heaven and earth is given unto him. He loves me, and died to save me, so that I may know that he will make all things work together for my good if I really love God. I will take every day's blessings and trials just as they come from Jesus' hands. He will order everything from hour to hour as I need. If I am in any trouble, I ought to look into my heart, and think over my actions, and see if there is not some wicked way in me, to which Jesus wants to call my attention. When I am happy in the enjoyment of God's goodness, I ought to remember *why* he shows such mercy to me. Dear Jesus, I owe all my blessings to thee. Grant that I may be always under thy gracious care! Amen.

SIXTH DAY.

For unto us a child is born, unto us a son is given: and the government shall be upon his shoulders: and his name shall be called Wonderful, Counsellor, The Mighty God, The Everlasting Father, The Prince of Peace. Is. ix. 6.

And when they were departed, behold, the angel of the Lord appeared to Joseph in a dream, saying, Arise, and take the young child and his mother, and flee into Egypt, and be thou there until I bring thee word: for Herod will seek the young child to destroy him. Matt. ii. 13.

In the beginning was the Word, and the Word was with God, and the Word was God. John i. 1.

And let all the angels of God worship him. Heb. i. 6.

Christ Jesus came into the world to save sinners. 1 Tim. i. 15.

I READ in the Bible that the holy Son of God became a child like me, and lived upon the earth. He came down from heaven,

FOR CHILDREN.

25

where he had always been with God from eternity. He was God, and the blessed angels and the holy spirits loved and worshipped him, and rejoiced to do his will. Why did he leave those holy beings and that happy place? Why did he come to this sinful world, and lie in the arms of Mary—a helpless babe? It is a wonderful thing to think of! Our earth seems so very far off from heaven, and we are all so unholy and miserable that it is very wonderful to me that the Saviour should come himself to live among us. If he had sent a beautiful angel to do us good, and to teach us how to please him, I should have thought that even such kindness was wonderful love. But he preferred to come *himself*, and be a little child, dependent upon Joseph and Mary for care and support. I suppose that he worked with his own hands with Joseph in his humble home. It does not surprise me that the angels desire to look into these things. The Bible says they do; and they sing louder and sweeter songs of praise to Jesus than we

DAILY MEDITATIONS

can, because they saw him in his glory before he left the skies to take upon him our nature. In one way they cannot love him, for he is not their Saviour. I will praise him because he lived and died for me.

Hark! hark! the notes of joy
    Roll o'er the heavenly plains,
And seraphs find employ
    For their sublimest strains;
Some new delight in heaven is known;
Loud sound the harps around the throne.

Hark! hark! the sound draws nigh,
    The joyful hosts descend;
Jesus forsakes the sky,
    To earth his footsteps bend;
He comes to bless our fallen race;
He comes with messages of grace.

Bear, bear the tidings round;
    Let every mortal know
What love in God is found,
    What pity he can show;
Ye winds that blow! ye waves that roll!
Bear the glad news from pole to pole.

FOR CHILDREN.

27

SEVENTH DAY.

The waters of Shiloah, that go softly. Is. viii. 6.

And as Jesus passed by, he saw a man which was blind from his birth.

And his disciples asked him, saying, Master, who did sin, this man, or his parents, that he was born blind ?

Jesus answered, Neither has this man sinned, nor his parents; but that the works of God should be made manifest in him.

I must work the works of him that sent me, while it is day; the night cometh, when no man can work.

As long as I am in the world, I am the light of the world.

When he had thus spoken, he spat on the ground, and made clay of the spittle, and he anointed the eyes of the blind man with the clay:

And said unto him, Go, wash in the pool of Siloam (which is by interpretation, Sent). He went his way therefore, and washed, and came seeing. John ix. 1–8.

DAILY MEDITATIONS

THE little brook Shiloah flowed softly and gently near the great and beautiful city of Jerusalem; its cool, clear water filled the pool of Siloam on the side of Mount Sion where the splendid temple stood. This was the pool in which the Saviour commanded the blind man to wash, that he might receive his sight. He bathed in waters which were led through channels cut in the solid rock underneath the holy city. God used this little bright and sparkling brook to give comfort and pleasure to all who went to the pool for refreshment. But the poor blind man must have been the happiest person who ever stepped out of that clear and healing water! He knew that it was the Lord who had opened his eyes, by a gracious miracle, and that the water itself could not have cured his blindness. Yet he must have loved often to visit that pool afterwards, and to remember the delight with which he first looked upon the beautiful world around him. Perhaps he used to go out of the city, and follow the little brook, as it wound around

FOR CHILDREN.

29

the hills. What loving thoughts of Jesus must have filled his heart!

May I not try to imitate even a brook, which makes itself a blessing to every one? A little child cannot do all that a grown person can, any more than the pretty brooks can be like great rivers, carrying noble ships, and watering whole continents. But still, the dear little brooks would be missed, by old and young, for they flow softly along, raising the heads of wild-flowers, and providing refreshment and pleasure for weary travellers and happy children. It is the love and sincerity we show, which makes our efforts to do good acceptable to others. If I wait till I can do some *great* thing, I'm afraid that I shall never do anything at all. O God, please to give me a willing heart, and show me, at all times and in every place, the ways in which I can do good, and the little acts of love and kindness, which thou wilt help me to perform. Amen.

DAILY MEDITATIONS

Oh, what can little hands do
To please the King of heaven?
The little hands some work may try
To help the poor in misery;—
Such grace to mine be given.

Oh, what can little lips do
To please the King of heaven?
The little lips can praise and pray,
And gentle words of kindness say;—
Such grace to mine be given.

Oh, what can little eyes do
To please the King of heaven?
The little eyes can upward look,
Can learn to read God's Holy Book;—
Such grace to mine be given.

Oh, what can little hearts do
To please the King of heaven?
Young hearts if God his spirit send,
Can love and trust their Saviour, Friend;-
Such grace to mine be given.

Though small is all that we can do
To please the King of heaven,
When hearts, and hands, and lips unite,
To serve the Saviour with delight,
They are most precious in his sight;—
Such grace to mine be given.

FOR CHILDREN.　31

EIGHTH DAY.

Not by works of righteousness which we have done, but according to his mercy he saved us. Titus iii. 5.

For whosoever shall keep the whole law, and yet offend in one point, he is guilty of all. .James ii. 10.

God hath given to us eternal life, and this life is in his Son.　1 John v. 11.

Even as the Son of man came not to be ministered unto, but to minister, and to give his life a ransom for many.　Matt. xx. 28.

I AM not told in God's Word, to do good works, that I may become righteous in his sight.　It would be very foolish and sinful for me to think that I could obtain the favour of the Great and Holy God, by even my best efforts to live a holy life.　It would be foolish in me to think so, because it would show how little I know what that holiness is which God's law requires of us;

DAILY MEDITATIONS

and it would be wicked, because God has said that all our righteousness is as filthy rags, and that he will not permit us to come into his presence, unless we are covered with the robe of righteousness which Jesus wrought.

But is the work all finished, and have I nothing to do but to enjoy God's blessings to me in this world, and to enter heaven when I die? I have found this verse, "God *hath* given to us eternal life,"—he gave it to us long ago, when Jesus lived and died to obtain it for us? He does not say that he *will* give it to us, if we bring to him a sufficient number of good works. Certainly he knew that we should never obtain eternal happiness through any merit of our own; and all that I can do is to accept the gift of life through Jesus Christ his Son.

I need not be searching for a treasure to pay my ransom with, for Jesus paid it long ago, with the price of his own precious blood. I need not try to pay it over again, with any works that I can do! Still I know

FOR CHILDREN.

that God commands us to be holy; and that he is pleased with our efforts to serve him. It is not wrong for me to tell him how I have tried to obey his commandments, and to fight against my sins. He will graciously accept my obedience, while I trust alone in the merits of Jesus for his favour. My feeble attempts to please him will be like fragrant flowers in his sight, though I may never be able to bring him any perfect fruit, to show my success in doing good works.

O God, help me to understand how to bring unto thee the righteousness of Christ by faith—for " without faith it is impossible " to please thee. Amen.

DAILY MEDITATIONS

34

NINTH DAY.

Can any hide himself in secret places that I shall not see him? saith the Lord. Jer. xxiii. 24.

And they heard the voice of the Lord God walking in the garden in the cool of the day: and Adam and his wife hid themselves from the presence of the Lord God, amongst the trees of the garden. Gen. iii. 8.

Thou compassest my path and my lying down, and art acquainted with all my ways. Ps. cxxxix. 11.

The Lord is at hand. Phil. iv. 5.

The Lord taketh pleasure in them that fear him, in those that hope in his mercy. Ps. cxlvii. 11.

For God hath power to help. 2 Chron. xxv. 8.

And therefore will the Lord wait, that he may be gracious unto you.

He will be very gracious unto thee at the voice of thy cry; when he shall hear it he will answer thee. Is. xxx. 18, 19.

FOR CHILDREN.

35

WHY should any one wish to flee from God's presence? It would be like wishing to get away from our best friend! Adam and Eve hid themselves among the trees of the garden, and dreaded to meet the Lord again, because they felt so ashamed and afraid after their disobedience. If it were not for our own sinful desires, I think we should rejoice to know that our heavenly Father is always near us.

Certainly it is God's love that leads him to attend us so constantly and mercifully. He does not act towards us as if he thought that our safety and happiness were of no consequence! When I think of his presence with me at all times, I will remember also his precious promises to those who depend upon him for all they wish or need. Does not God say that he waits to be gracious to us? In his infinite compassion he comes near to us, and bends his ear to listen to our prayers. He is always ready to stretch out his hand to help us when we are in danger, just as the Lord reached. forth his arm to

DAILY MEDITATIONS

save Peter from sinking in the water. I am glad to know that I can never go out of his sight; that he is for ever by my side to know my condition. I do not believe that he stands by us always to watch for our faults and our sins, that he may write them down in his book, or punish us as we deserve! It is much pleasanter to think that he follows us to guide and help us, and that he has precious gifts in his hands for us, if we will only ask him to bestow upon us these good things.

Oh yes; it is sweet to think of God's power and love, while we remember that he is always near us! He can do for us all that we need; and if I look to him to keep me in the right way he will hear my prayer. It will please him to have me depend upon his love.

FOR CHILDREN. 37

TENTH DAY.

A lively hope.   1 Pet. i. 3.

The hope of eternal life.   Titus iii. 7.

How then shall they call on him in whom they have not believed? and how shall they believe in him of whom they have not heard? and how shall they hear without a preacher? Rom. x. 14.

Having no hope, and without God in the world.   Eph. ii. 12.

I HAVE found in the Bible this expression—"a lively hope;" and one of my friends has told me that it means *a hope of life*. It seems to me to contain a great deal that is precious to think of, in a few words. I know that it does not mean a hope of life in this world, though I am sure that if I was in any danger, and expected to die, and a hope of life were given to me, I should be very grateful and happy. It means *the hope of everlasting life*, which God has given us —the hope that we have through Jesus that

DAILY MEDITATIONS

our souls shall live with God in heaven after our lives in this world are over.

If it were not for the Bible and the precious Saviour, we should know nothing of the future. We should be like the poor heathen, who have no knowledge of God and heaven. How sad it is to think of the thousands of wretched and ignorant people who live in lands where the Gospel is never preached! Of course they cannot worship or love a being about whom they know nothing. They have no Bible to tell them of the life of the soul; and they have only a little light in their own hearts, by which to see the difference between what is right and wrong! Oh, I should like to tell them how the Saviour was crucified for us! I should like to tell them about the beautiful place we call heaven, where we hope to see Jesus, and live for ever with those who love him! When I am older, perhaps God will want me to go into some heathen country, and be a missionary to those who have no " hope of life!"

FOR CHILDREN.

39

Am I not like the blind man, whose eyes were opened to see Jesus; and shall I not do all I can to have others see and love him too? I need not wait till I am grown, to be a missionary, for we are all missionaries so long as we are in this world. We are all sent into the world *to do something*, and a missionary only means "one who is sent." God has sent me into the world, and I must be *his* missionary—to do his work.

God is the Creator and Father of all the many millions of people upon the earth. We are all made in his image, and our souls are just alike in his sight. Why has he put such a difference between me and the poor heathen? When I remember all his mercies to me, and all my advantages, I am ashamed to think how little I love him. I will offer to God the prayer that Paul did—"Lord, what wilt thou have *me* to do?"

DAILY MEDITATIONS

ELEVENTH DAY.

For the Son of man is come to seek and save that which was lost. Luke xix. 10.

And he spake this parable unto them saying, What man of you, having an hundred sheep, if he lose one of them, doth not leave the ninety and nine in the wilderness, and go after that which is lost, until he find it?

And when he hath found it, he layeth it on his shoulders, rejoicing.

And when he cometh home, he calleth together his friends and neighbours, saying unto them, Rejoice with me; for I have found my sheep which was lost.

I say unto you, That likewise joy shall be in heaven over one sinner that repenteth, more than over ninety and nine just persons which need no repentance.

Either what woman, having ten pieces of silver, if she lose one piece, doth not light a candle, and sweep the house, and seek diligently till she find it?

FOR CHILDREN.

41

And when she hath found it, she calleth her friends and her neighbours together, saying, Rejoice with me; for I have found the piece which I had lost.

Likewise, I say unto you, There is joy in the presence of the angels of God over one sinner that repenteth. Luke xv. 3–11.

I have gone astray like a lost sheep. Ps. cxix. 176.

I DO not remember that I was ever lost so that I could not find my way back to my home. And I can scarcely imagine how distressed and frightened I should be if I were far away from my father's house without any one to help me to return. It must be a dreadful thing to be *lost*. And yet the Bible speaks of Jesus the Redeemer as of one who came "to seek and to save *the lost*." Did he not come to save us all? Who are "the lost"? Does it not mean that we have wandered out of the way which leads to our heavenly home? It must be that Jesus means to tell us that God is our Father, and that we are like poor, lonely, disobedient children, who have chosen to give up his love, and to try to find our happiness in sinful pleasures and among wicked companions. This is being lost from the way of holiness; it is being far away from the dear Saviour's arms; it is being *lost* amidst the sins and dangers to which Satan is ever trying to lead us. He does not wish to see us holy and happy, and therefore he tempts us to forget God, and to wander away from the safe and pleasant paths in which Jesus would have us walk.

Surely I am one of the "lost" whom Jesus came to seek and save. But I think he is near me now, asking me let him guide me and to let him teach me. I do not wish to live away from him—separated from him by my sins. I will tell him that I am lost, and that I trust in him to lead me back to my heavenly Father's love, because he came to seek and save the lost.

FOR CHILDREN.

43

TWELFTH DAY.

And when he had spoken these things, while they beheld, he was taken up; and a cloud received him out of their sight.

And, while they looked steadfastly toward heaven as he went up, behold, two men stood by them in white apparel.

Which also said, Ye men of Galilee, why stand ye gazing up into heaven? this same Jesus, which is taken up from you into heaven, shall so come in like manner as ye have seen him go into heaven. Acts i. 9, 10, 11.

I AM surprised that the two men in white. apparel should have asked the disciples why they stood gazing up into heaven! Had not the dear Saviour just gone up into the clouds? I do not wonder that they stood looking up so steadfastly! It must have broken their hearts with grief to have Jesus leave them so suddenly! And then they understood so little about heaven and

DAILY MEDITATIONS

about what Jesus could do for them there! They knew very well that here in this wicked world the enemies of the Lord would try to persecute and kill them. How discouraging and alarming it must have been to them to be left alone without the protection of their glorious and precious Master. Perhaps Jesus thought that this feeling of loneliness and fear would lead them to pray unto him, and to tell him all their troubles. He wanted, I suppose, to teach them to live by faith upon his love and strength. When they saw him right by their side it was easy to depend upon him, because he did such wonderful things to show them his power and willingness to protect and to bless those who trusted in him. And often he had let them know that he could read their thoughts and see just what they needed without being near to them, so that they could see him. I am sure that they ought to have known that he could be their friend and helper up in the skies the same as when he was with them

FOR CHILDREN.

45

upon the earth! But they were so astonished by his rising into the air and disappearing from their sight, that they could not think of these things. No doubt, many things which Jesus had said were brought to their remembrance after the Holy Spirit came down, which Jesus had promised to send into their hearts. But the two men comforted them by telling them that the same dear Saviour they loved should come again in the clouds from heaven to take them to be with him for ever. Shall I see this glorious sight? Oh! that I may live in the presence of Jesus now by faith, so that I may not be terrified when I see him coming again with all the holy angels through the skies.

46 DAILY MEDITATIONS

THIRTEENTH DAY.

Now when Jesus was born in Bethlehem of Judea, in the days of Herod the king, behold, there came wise men from the east to Jerusalem,

Saying, Where is he that is born King of the Jews? for we have seen his star in the east, and are come to worship him.

When Herod the king had heard these things, he was troubled, and all Jerusalem with him.

And when he had gathered all the chief priests and scribes of the people together, he demanded of them where Christ should be born.

And they said unto him, In Bethlehem of Judea: for thus it is written by the prophet,

And thou, Bethlehem, in the land of Juda, art not the least among the princes of Juda : for out of thee shall come a Governor, that shall rule my people Israel.

Then Herod, when he had privily called the wise men, inquired of them diligently what time the time the star appeared.

And he sent them to Bethlehem, and said,

FOR CHILDREN.

47

Go and search diligently for the young child; and when ye have found him, bring me word again, that I may come and worship him also.

When they had heard the king, they departed; and, lo, the star, which they saw in the east, went before them, till it came and stood over where the child was.

When they saw the star, they rejoiced with exceeding great joy.

And when they were come into the house, they saw the young child with Mary his mother, and fell down and worshipped him: and when they had opened their treasures, they presented unto him gifts; gold, and frankincense, and myrrh. Matt. ii. 1–11.

THE wise men from the east were very curious to see the holy babe which was born King of the Jews. They followed the star which God put in the heavens to guide them to the place where Jesus was; and when they came to the stable in which the holy child was born they presented unto him gifts, gold, and frankincense, and myrrh. I cannot help wondering what Mary did

DAILY MEDITATIONS

with all these rich and beautiful things which the wise men gave to the little babe. But I know that God had shown to these great men that this little child was his Son, and that he was the Messiah whom they had so long expected. They knew that they ought to bow down and worship him. It was the custom in their country to carry precious gifts to their earthly king, and so they tried to please the Lord by offering to him these valuable presents as a proof of their adoration and joy. They rejoiced because they were allowed to see and welcome the promised Saviour.

Would it not be pleasant to take some little gift to the Lord, and ask him to let it remind him of our love? Yes, I think it would. But he does not need anything that we can bring him! There is only one thing which he asks us to give to him. He does say, "Give me thy heart." Oh, how can I offer him such an unholy and sinful thing? Yet, I will ask him to take my heart at once, for I know that he wants me

FOR CHILDREN. 49

to give it to him that he may wash it and make it holy. Dear Jesus, I have nothing else to bring thee but my poor, sinful heart; please to accept it.

Jesus, who on Calvary's mountain
　　Poured thy precious blood for me,
Wash me in its flowing fountain,
　　That my soul may spotless be.

I have sinned, but oh, restore me;
　　For unless thou smile on me,
Dark is all the world before me,
　　Darker yet eternity!

In thy word I hear thee saying,
　　Come and I will give you rest;
And the gracious call obeying,
　　See, I hasten to thy breast,

Grant, oh, grant, thy Spirit's teaching,
　　That I may not go astray,
Till the gate of heaven reaching,
　　Earth and sin are passed away.

D

FOURTEENTH DAY.

For one star differeth from another star in glory. 1 Cor. xv. 41.

Be ye followers of me, even as I am of Christ. 1 Cor. xi. 1.

Fear not, neither be discouraged. Deut. i. 21.

For I have given you an example. John xiii. 15.

Ye are our epistles written in our hearts, known and read of all men. 2 Cor. iii. 2.

I MIGHT spend whole days trying to find two leaves exactly alike, and I should not succeed! I might listen for hours in a forest to hear the same song from two different birds, and I should not hear it! It would be impossible even for me to find two birds with the same plumage! Each landscape is different from every other, and no two human faces are just alike. God has given us a great deal of pleasure in just the variety in things around us! It is a comfort to me to think that God intended to have all this dif-

FOR CHILDREN.

51

ference in the same kind of things. Sometimes when I read the memoirs of good children I think that God would be better satisfied with me if I were like them, and then it comforts me to think about the birds and the leaves and the different flowers. The roses and the lilies are very different, yet God made them both, and they please him, I think, all the more because they are not alike. When I read the lives and history of those who have loved Jesus, I will try to imitate them so far as they pleased the Lord; but I will not be discouraged because I cannot be exactly like them, nor do exactly the same things.

I will ask the Holy Spirit to help me to study the life and example of Jesus, who became a child, and grew up to be a man that we might have a perfect pattern by which we should live. We have in the Bible a description of him, in order that we may try to imitate him in all that we can. The books and letters in the Bible teaching us the character of our dear Saviour are very precious. They were written by men who died long ago, and

I must remember that it is my duty to be a *living letter*, which may be known and read by all men, just as they would read the character of Jesus in one of those old and precious letters written so long ago. I must try to show in my own life what Jesus wishes us to be. O God, help me to grow more and more like Jesus, and give me grace to follow his example. Amen.

> Behold, where in a mortal form
>   Appears each grace divine:
> The virtues, all in Jesus met,
>   With mildest radiance shine.
>
> Be Christ our pattern and our guide;
>   His image may we bear;
> Oh may we tread his holy steps,
>   His joy and glory share!

FIFTEENTH DAY.

The answer of a good conscience toward God.
1 Pet. iii. 21.

A pure conscience. 1 Tim. iii. 3–9.

An evil conscience. Heb. x. 22.

Having their conscience seared with a hot iron.
1 Tim. iv. 2.

Convicted by their own conscience. John
viii. 9.

Yea, and why even of yourselves judge ye not
what is right? Luke xii. 57.

And thou shalt do that which is right and good
in the sight of the Lord. Deut. vi. 18.

To seek of him a right way for us. Ezra viii. 21.

A still small voice. 1 Kings xix. 12.

Behold the Lamb of God, which taketh away
the sins of the world. John i. 29.

Cast thy burden upon the Lord. Ps. lv. 22.

GOD has given to each of us a conscience,
to help us to decide whether our thoughts
and wishes are right or wrong. There is

DAILY MEDITATIONS

54

something within us which seems to talk with us and try to influence us to do right. It is surely God's voice in our hearts, and it must be very dangerous and wicked for me to disregard it. We have the holy rules by which we are to govern our conduct,.written very plainly in the Bible; and, besides this written law, when we wish to do anything, our consciences judge whether it will please God or not. What if the judge within us should not decide correctly about our actions, or should not speak to us at all; when we are very much tempted to sin, is there not danger that we shall not hear God's still small voice in our hearts? How dreadful it would be if we were left to our own choice and will! We could never get away from temptations, and there would be nothing within us to help us to resist the sinful desires which would soon destroy our souls.

And every time I commit a sin, they say it makes the voice of God feebler and fainte· within me. O God, let me never try to silence my conscience! Let me not wickedly

FOR CHILDREN.

55

persist in my wrong-doings! Put into my heart a fear of thine anger and of thy judgments, and keep my conscience awake, to warn me instantly of the approach of the tempter. Make me afraid of even the smallest sins—for I know that thou hatest all sin.

Will my conscience remind me of those duties I have neglected to do? will it help me to repent of my sins of omission? Yes, I am told that God will educate and enlighten this conscience which speaks for him in my heart, so that it will reprove me for neglecting to perform my duty. The Holy Spirit is the keeper and instructor of my inward judge; he can make my conscience sensitive and tender and faithful and honest. I will pray for such a conscience.

But oh, who can take the burden of my sins away? Who can bear to think of all the wrong acts of his life? My conscience will keep me unhappy all the time, if I let it show me all my faults! The sinfulness of my heart is very painful to me! Dear Jesus, I bring all my burden to thee; please to open

the windows of my dark and sinful soul, and
let me look out to the sunshine of thy love.
Amen.

There is a little lonely fold,
  Whose flock one Shepherd keeps,
Through summer's heat and winter's cold,
  With eye that never sleeps.

By evil beast, or burning sky,
  Or damp of midnight air,
Not one in all that flock shall die
  Beneath that Shepherd's care.

For if, unheeding or beguiled,
  In danger's path they roam,
His pity follows through the wild,
  And guards them safely home.

O gentle Shepherd, still behold
  Thy helpless charge in me;
And take a wanderer to thy fold,
  That trembling turns to thee!

FOR CHILDREN.

57

SIXTEENTH DAY.

Truly the light is sweet, and a pleasant thing it is for the eyes to behold the sun. Eccl. xi. 7.

As for these four children, God gave them knowledge and skill in all learning and wisdom. Dan. i. 17.

But the path of the just is as the shining light, that shineth more and more unto the perfect day.

The way of the wicked is as darkness, they know not at what they stumble. Prov. iv. 18, 19.

I am come a light into the world, that whosoever believeth on me should not abide in darkness. John xii. 46.

Let your light so shine among men, that they may see your good works, and glorify your Father which is in heaven. Matt. v. 16.

I DO not like to sit in a dark room, or to walk where I have no light. It is very unpleasant, and I am afraid of stumbling in the darkness. If I'm sleeping I do not need or wish the light, but when I am awake I

DAILY MEDITATIONS

enjoy the sunshine; and I think that God made my eyes so that the light should be sweet and pleasant to me. I could not enjoy the beautiful things which God has made, if it were always dark around me; and I could never see the faces of my friends! O God, I thank thee for the bright and cheerful light!

But there is another kind of light besides that which shines from the sun and the moon and the stars. There is light for our minds as well as for our eyes,—knowledge is called light. How very little of this kind of light there is in my mind! Still I will not be discouraged, for I know that the sun gradually drives away the darkness in the morning till it is perfectly light. The more I study and observe things around me, the more light of knowledge I shall have; and my mind will grow stronger as I grow older. I will pray for God's blessing on my mind, that I may learn that which is useful, and know the difference between good and evil.

And there is still another kind of light, for

FOR CHILDREN.

Jesus says, "I am the light of the world; he that followeth me shall not walk in darkness, but shall have the light of life." This is the light I need the most! If I believe in Jesus and love him, then the light of God's grace has begun to shine in my heart, and it will increase more and more, till I am made holy and happy in the light of my heavenly Father's love and smile. This glorious light which Jesus gives does indeed "shine in a dark place," and the beginning of a holy life, the Bible calls the rising of a "day-star" in our hearts.

Dear Jesus, come, I pray thee, and bring thy light into my soul, that I may love thee more, and please thee better. Amen.

DAILY MEDITATIONS

SEVENTEENTH DAY.

I have finished the work which thou gavest me to do. John xvii. 4.

Boast not thyself of to-morrow; for thou knowest not what a day may bring forth. Prov. xxvii. 1.

Therefore are they before the throne of God, and serve him day and night in his temple. Rev. vii. 15.

I will help thee. Is. xli. 10.

I HAVE made up my mind that God will not be pleased if I do nothing but *play*. There certainly is some kind of *work* which he expects me to do, and I must try and find out what it is, and begin to do it; for no one else can do *my* work, and if I neglect to do it, it will surely be left undone. Shall all the rest of the world be busy and I be idle? No; I should be ashamed to leave this earth and go up to my heavenly Father without finishing the work which he gave me to do.

FOR CHILDREN.

61

What *can* a child like me do? Certainly most of my work must be done at home, by my dear mother's side, and among my brothers and sisters! I shall have to be constantly watching to see what my duty is, for it is only little things which I can do, and if I am careless I shall not notice them, and then my work will not be done.

I must not put off till to-morrow what I ought to do to-day, for to-morrow I shall have no time to spare. There will be something for me to do to-morrow which I did not see or think of to-day, and I cannot take the time for my neglected work.

But I cannot work all the time! It tires me whenever I try to see how much I can do! Besides, I like to play; and mother tells me that God likes to have me enjoy myself with my friends, and that playing will help me to work all the better. How sweet it is to think that Jesus watches us at our play! I will try not to play anything that would displease or offend him. It seems to me that play ought not to be called idleness;

DAILY MEDITATIONS

because if it does me good, then it is a part of my work. There will never come a day which I may spend in idleness, and think that I have nothing to do. In heaven God will give to each of us holy work to do, and we shall have better powers with which to serve him.

This I will remember—that my heavenly Father has not only given me my particular work, but he also offers to help me to do it.

Do thy best always—do it now—
    For in the present time,
As in the furrows of a plow,
    Fall seeds of good or crime.

The sun and rain will ripen fast
    Each seed that thou hast sown,
And every act and word at last
    By its own fruit be known.

And soon the harvest of thy toil,
    Rejoicing, thou shalt reap;
Or o'er thy wild neglected soil,
    Go forth in shame to weep.

FOR CHILDREN.

EIGHTEENTH DAY.

Whoso putteth his trust in the Lord shall be safe.   Prov. xxix. 25.

I will not fail thee nor forsake thee.   Josh. i. 15.

I will surely do thee good.   Gen. xxxii. 12.

I pray not that thou shouldest take them out of the world, but that thou shouldest keep them from the evil.   John xvii. 15.

And we know that all things work together for good to them that love God.   Rom. viii. 29.

The hand of our God is upon all them for good that seek him; but his power and his wrath is against all them that forsake him.   Ezra viii. 22.

SAFE! Yes; I am perfectly safe in my heavenly Father's care! He will not forget me; he will not forget that I am weak, and helpless to take care of myself; he will not forget to supply my wants, and to protect me from danger! In thee, dear heavenly Father, do I put my trust; for I know that thou art willing a little child should trust in thee, and thou art able to do for me more than I can ask or think.

If God is my friend, I need not fear anything which shall happen. I will not be afraid of the evil which Jesus says is in the world; nor of Satan, who tries to destroy my soul by tempting me to sin. I will be afraid of nothing, for God's power can deliver me from everything which can harm or injure me. We are safe because we belong to our faithful Saviour, Jesus Christ; and no enemy can pluck us from his hands. No one can take from us the blessings that God gives us, or hinder him from doing as good. God is a great King, and he will not suffer any one to take away the peace of those who serve him.

But if I am outside of the heavenly fold, like a lost sheep lying out in the open field, I shall be exposed to every danger. God's protecting arm will not be around me here in this world, nor in the long eternity through which my soul must live. This is a dreadful thought—that God will not be my

FOR CHILDREN. 65

friend nor my protector. If I hate sin and love holiness, and trust in Jesus to save my soul, then all things in God's great universe shall bring me happiness. But if I reject the Saviour's love, and go on in my sinful ways, then no sweet assurances of God's love shall bless me, but everything will be dark and sad, and bring me the punishment I deserve.

O God, do not let me forget thy power to punish, as well as thy gracious power to do us good. Keep me, I beseech thee, under thy protecting wings for ever! Amen.

Since, with pure and firm affection,
Thou on God hast set thy love,
With the wings of his protection
He will shield thee from above;
Thou shalt call on him in trouble,
He will hearken, he will save;
Here, for grief, reward thee double,
Crown with life beyond the grave.

66 *DAILY MEDITATIONS*

NINETEENTH DAY.

Behold, happy is the man whom God correcteth. Job v. 17.

For whom the Lord loveth he correcteth; even as a father the son in whom he delighteth. Prov. iii. 12.

As many as I love, I rebuke and chasten; be zealous therefore, and repent. Rev. iii. 19.

WHEN the beautiful flowers are all faded, and the leaves have fallen from the trees, and the earth is covered with snow, it seems as if God were angry with us and had taken away a great many pleasures and comforts from us! We shiver in the cold, and everything looks dreary. But then, though we cannot see God's gentle hand working so silently beneath the snow and ice, we know that he is preparing for us the beauty of the Spring, and the blessings of the fruitful months. It *seems* as if God had put a cold and frozen band around our dear pleasant

FOR CHILDREN.

67

earth, when *really* it is his kind and loving arm working wonders for us, about which we can know but very little.

Well, sometimes my heart seems just like a garden from which all the birds have flown, and in which all the flowers have faded. I feel as if all that made me happy had been taken away. And because God, my heavenly Father, sees it best to send me disappointments, or to let me suffer pain, I say to myself, God is making it all winter in my heart, and taking away the pleasant things I enjoyed. Oh, how little I know of God's compassion! How ready I am to complain! Are we not told in the Bible that the way to heaven is narrow and straight—a way in which but few love to walk? Why do I not oftener think of the *end* of this heavenly way?

When I am sick or in any trouble I ought not to think that God does not love me; even though I can see that he is punishing me for my sins. Will he not be more like a father to those who wish to be his chil-

68 *DAILY MEDITATIONS*

dren, than to those who do not love him? And certainly if he loves us he will reprove our faults. He is very tender in his care of us! He notices all our troubles and trials, and he stands beside us in the midst of all the things which so constantly disturb us. I'm sure he would rejoice to smooth the rough places in our journey to heaven if it were always for our good. But sometimes we need these unpleasant things to remind us that this beautiful earth is not our home, and that we must hasten on our heavenly way, without loving our pleasures here so much as to make us forget the life which is eternal. Thus God shows us, that his tenderest compassion and love is for our souls, and if we are patient under his corrections, we shall be better prepared for the enjoyments of our heavenly home.

> Thy way, not mine, O Lord!
>   However dark it be;
> Lead me by thine own hand,
>   Choose out the path for me.

FOR CHILDREN.

Smooth let it be or rough,
   It will be still the best ;
Winding or straight, it matters not,
   It leads me to thy rest.

I dare not choose my lot,
   I would not, if I might ;
Choose thou for me, my God,
   So shall I walk aright.

Choose thou for me my friends,
   My sickness or my health ;
Choose thou my cares for me,
   My poverty or wealth.

Take thou my cup, and it
   With joy or sorrow fill,
 As best to thee may seem ;
   Choose thou my good and ill.

DAILY MEDITATIONS

TWENTIETH DAY.

For what is your life? It is even a vapour, that appeareth for a little time, and then vanisheth away. James iv. 14.

My days are swifter than a weaver's shuttle. Job vii. 6.

Whatsoever thy hand findeth to do, do it with thy might; for there is no work, nor device, nor knowledge, nor wisdom, in the grave whither thou goest. Eccl. ix. 10.

For the things which are seen are temporal; but the things which are not seen are eternal. 2 Cor. iv. 18.

ANOTHER day has gone! I am one day nearer to the close of my earthly life! Who knows what shall happen before the sun rises again? No one can tell what a day may bring forth. One thing is certain—our whole life, though it may seem long to us, is but a little day in God's sight! And the night of death comes nearer and nearer as each day's sun goes down.

FOR CHILDREN.

God will inquire at the end of this earthly day, what I have done. He does not expect us to be idle or to live for ourselves alone. There is something for me to do in each day as it passes, and in every place where I am. The most important work I have to do is to prepare myself for death and heaven. My mind seems always filled with the thoughts and pleasures of this world; I suppose it is because I am constantly in the midst of its scenes. How can I think as I ought of those things which are *unseen?* It is just as if I were sitting at a window with a tree between me and the landscape beyond—I should see nothing but the tree, because it was so near me. O God, open the eyes of my mind to see the things of the next world just as they are; and though the things of this world are near and close around, let me not forget the better life beyond this earthly one!

These bodies for which we do so much, will soon be carried by our friends to the quiet grave! How many plans I make for to-morrow, and how little I think of what I shall do in eternity! It is foolish and dangerous for me to live so forgetful of my eternal life. My dear parents are always telling me to learn *now* the things I shall need to know when I am grown. They say that I must prepare myself for my future life in this world now while I am a child. Does not God call our earthly life our childhood; and must I not prepare in time for eternity? If I expect to enjoy heaven, surely I must try to fit myself to associate with the holy beings who are there.

When each day's scenes and labours close,
And wearied nature seeks repose,
With pardoning mercy richly blest,
Guard me, my Saviour, while I rest!
And as each morning sun shall rise,
Oh, lead me onward to the skies!

And at my life's last setting sun,
My conflicts o'er, my labours done,
Jesus! thy heavenly radiance shed,
To cheer and bless my dying bed—
And from death's gloom my spirit raise,
To see thy face, and sing thy praise.

FOR CHILDREN.

73

TWENTY-FIRST DAY.

What would ye that I should do for you? Mark x. 36.

The Lord is good unto them that wait for him, to the soul that seeketh him.   Lam. iii. 25.

No good thing will he withhold from them that walk uprightly.   Ps. lxxxiv. 11.

The Lord giveth wisdom.   Prov. ii. 6.

Watch and pray, that ye enter not into temptation.   Matt. xxvi. 41.

He forgetteth not the cry of the humble.   Ps. ix. 12.

If ye shall ask anything in my name, I will do it.   John xiv. 14.

And the Lord hath given me my petition which I asked of him.   1 Sam. i. 27.

Before they call I will answer; and while they are yet speaking I will hear.   Is. lxv. 24.

HOW many times have I written to my parents when I was absent from home, asking them to send me certain things!

DAILY MEDITATIONS

How anxiously I waited for answers to my letters. And when they gratified my wishes, how glad and grateful I was! How soon I returned my thanks to my dear, kind parents! Oh, if I could only have the same confidence in my heavenly Father's love and his willingness to hear and bless me! If I could only go directly to him and ask for the things which I need! How delightful it would be to feel that God welcomes my prayer just as my parents delight to have me go to them with my requests!

Certainly God has said, " Ask, and ye shall receive." I will reverently carry this promise to him when I kneel to pray, and then I will not pretend to want blessings which I feel no real desire in my heart to have. I will, above all things, be sincere in God's holy presence. I will not mock him with a prayer for his Holy Spirit to keep me from sin, when I do not wish or intend to be holy. I will not offer before his glorious throne praises which do not rise with gratitude from my heart. I will not insult

FOR CHILDREN.

the infinite God with a prayer which I do not remember even for a day.

When my heavenly Father invites me to ask for what I need, I will go into his presence with humility, and offer unto him my petitions in the name of Jesus, who pleads for us before his Father's throne.

I would be solemn and earnest while I talk with God; but I will not be afraid to tell him that I love him, for he is willing to listen to the prayers and praises of the youngest and simplest. Does he not say, " Let me hear thy voice "?

Let me thank God that my sins cannot be too many or too great for his mercy to pardon. Therefore, I will confess my sins daily to him, and strive not to repeat the wickedness which offends him. I will also tell the Lord of all my temptations. My prayers shall be like my letters to my earthly parents. I will look for God's gracious answers, and I will rejoice to return my thanks for his goodness and love.

DAILY MEDITATIONS

Come, my soul, thy suit prepare,
Jesus loves to answer prayer;
He himself has bid thee pray,
Therefore will not say thee nay.

Thou art coming to a king,
Large petitions with thee bring;
For his grace and power are such,
None can ever ask too much.

With my burden I begin:
Lord, remove this load of sin!
Let thy blood, for sinners spilt,
Set my conscience free from guilt.

While I am a pilgrim here,
Let thy love my spirit cheer;
As my Guide, my Guard, my Friend,
Lead me to my journey's end.

Show me what I have to do,
Every hour my strength renew;
Let me live a life of faith,
Let me die thy people's death.

FOR CHILDREN.　　77

TWENTY-SECOND DAY.

For whosoever exalteth himself shall be abased and he that humbleth himself shall be exalted. Luke xiv. 11.

And those that walk in pride He is able to abase.　Dan. iv. 37.

Talk no more so exceeding proudly; let not arrogancy come out of your mouth : for the Lord is a God of knowledge, and by him actions are weighed.　1 Sam. ii. 3.

Choose the things that please me.　Is. lxv. 4.

And the patriarchs, moved with envy, sold Joseph into Egypt.　Acts vii. 9.

Let us not be desirous of vainglory, provoking one another, envying one another.　Gal. v. 26.

Let nothing be done through strife or vainglory; but in lowliness of mind let each esteem other better than themselves.　Phil. ii. 3.

EVERYBODY praises the sun! Grown people and children, and birds and animals are glad and happy in the light and

DAILY MEDITATIONS

warmth which the glorious sun pours down upon everything and every creature on the earth! But who ever thought of the sun's being proud? The flowers bloom in beautiful shapes and colours everywhere, and everybody admires and loves them—but who ever called the flowers proud? The dear little birds all day long sing the sweetest songs in our gardens and in the solemn forests—but did any one ever say that the birds were vain and proud? Oh, no; the sun doesn't care whether we raise our eyes or not to look at his golden face. The flowers will spring up in places where their beautiful leaves will never be seen. The happy birds will sing whether any one listens or not! Neither the sun, nor the flowers, nor the birds are proud of what they are or of what they can do!

To be sure, pride is very wicked and very foolish! but I cannot think that it is wrong for me to be glad when I please others, and see that they love me. It must be right for us to try to please others and to gain their

FOR CHILDREN.

79

love. Yet I have often been made unhappy by desiring too much the praise of my friends. I have been disappointed when they neglected to approve my looks and conduct. And besides all this foolishness, I am afraid I have sometimes been envious of the praise and admiration betowed upon others. This certainly is wicked pride, and it must be one of the evil things which proceed out of my heart. O God, please to take this unholy spirit away from me!

Do I not sometimes wish so much for the praise of others, and for their good opinion of me, that I pretend to be what I really am not? How hateful this must be in the sight of God, who reads our hearts! Dear heavenly Father, let thy grace in my heart be like the roots of a vine, which go down deep into the earth, so that there may be the real fruits of holiness in my daily life.

Is it not wicked pride which makes us think that we are free from the faults others have? Are we not forbidden to compare ourselves with others at all? It will be safest for me to study God's commands, and then I shall see what my character is, and I shall be able to know whether my conduct is such as to please him. I ought to pray, and strive most of all to please God!

If I remember my many advantages, with all the instruction I have received, it will humble my pride to see how little progress I have made, and how little there is to admire in me. I will try not to be proud, or dependent upon the praise of others. But yet I will offer to God my thanks for the love of my friends, and for the pleasure I have in trying to please them.

'Tis *being*, and *doing*,
And *having*, that make
All the pleasures and pains
Of which beings partake :
To *be* what God pleases—
To *do* a man's best;
And to *have* a good heart—
Is the way to be blest.

FOR CHILDREN. 81

TWENTY-THIRD DAY.

For there is not a word in my tongue, but, lo, O Lord, thou knowest it altogether. Ps. cxxxix. 4.

As we have therefore opportunity, let us do good unto all men. Gal. vi. 10.

Honour all men. 1 Pet. ii. 7.

And the King shall answer and say unto them, Verily I say unto you, inasmuch as ye have done it unto one of the least of these my brethren, ye have done it unto me. Matt. xxv. 40.

And this is his commandment, That we should believe on the name of his Son Jesus Christ, and love one another, as he gave us commandment. 1 John iii. 23.

I WONDER if there were any children in Nazareth or Jerusalem who were rude or uncivil or disrespectful to Jesus; if there were any who were rough and noisy and ill-behaved in his presence. I cannot bear to think that any boy or girl would insult and grieve him by such impolite and vulgar

F

DAILY MEDITATIONS

conduct! And now, while I am thinking about it, it seems to me that such behaviour towards any person must displease him just as much as if it were offered to himself. Our unkind looks and rough voices must grieve him though he is so far away. Was not the expression upon his face always gentle, and gracious, and kind? He was full of grace and kindness when he dwelt among men. His voice was mild and full of love, and it seems to me that no one could have looked up into his eyes without wanting to kneel down at his feet—to praise and worship him. And does he not say that a kindness shown to any of his friends is a kindness done to himself? Oh, will he not consider all our rude and disrespectful conduct to others as offered to himself?

We cannot love everybody alike! Did not the Lord appear to love John best, when he let him lean his head upon his bosom, at the supper in the upper room? Surely he must be willing that we should

FOR CHILDREN.

have our particular friends. But certainly we ought to feel kindly towards every one, and to be glad to do them good as often as we have opportunity. If we were all really interested in each other's happiness, what a pleasant world it would be! How glad we should be to see each other; and how easily the cheerfulness and kindness of our hearts would be discovered in our words and tones!

When I feel ill-natured and selfish, I will try more than ever to put on a pleasant face, and to speak with a pleasant tone and manner; for mother says if I strive to *act* politely and properly, it will help me to *feel* kindly; but that if I yield at all to impatience, or selfishness, or anger, I shall only increase the difficulty of overcoming the wrong feeling.

Does it not show the wickedness of our hearts, when God has to command us to be respectful and kind? How strange that we should have to be *commanded* to love each other!

DAILY MEDITATIONS

TWENTY-FOURTH DAY.

There is joy in the presence of the angels of God over one sinner that repenteth. Luke xv. 10.

Oh the depth of the riches both of the wisdom and knowledge of God! How unsearchable are his judgments, and his ways past finding out! Rom. xi. 33.

For who maketh thee to differ from another? 1 Cor. iv. 7.

What shall I render unto the Lord for all his benefits toward me? Ps. cxvi. 12.

The Lord maketh poor, and maketh rich; he bringeth low, and lifteth up. 1 Sam. ii. 8.

Did not I weep for him that was in trouble? Was not my soul grieved for the poor? Job xxx. 25.

Blessed is he that considereth the poor; the Lord will deliver him in time of trouble. Ps. xli. 1.

AS the angels look down from heaven upon our round green earth, I suppose that it appears a very little world to them!

FOR CHILDREN.

85

They could easily count all the members of God's great family who live here! What feelings of surprise and wonder they must have as they look into our different homes! How much darkness and ignorance and wretchedness they would see among the people in some parts of the world! With what joy they would look into Christian homes, and listen to the hymns which the friends of Jesus sing! How could they help wondering why God put such a difference between his earthly children? Would they not long to make us feel the greatness of God's sovereign goodness to us? Would they not like to tell us how he sits a glorious King upon his throne, giving gifts to those whom he selects to receive his bounty, and guiding and ordering all things in love and wisdom?

When they saw a little infant laid in the arms of loving parents, who were able to give it a warm and happy home; when they saw its little soul committed to the care of a father and mother who would delight in

86 DAILY MEDITATIONS

leading it to Jesus—would they not rejoice in the love and mercy of God? And when they saw another dear little babe given to a heathen mother, or left in a poor and wretched home — would they not weep, though they know that God is wise and good in all that he does? I think his ways must be unsearchable and past finding out, even to angels!

Oh, why has it pleased God to do so much for me? How can I praise him enough that he gave me such parents and such a cheerful and happy home! How many poor children are without friends to provide them shelter, or food, or clothing! It must be very hard to be poor! May I never forget those to whom God has denied the blessings he has given to me; let me try to think of them in their cheerless homes till I am ready to deny myself pleasures to do them good!

Surely God's kindness to me ought to make me willing and glad to return to him the most grateful obedience. He asks us to

FOR CHILDREN. 87

consider what great things he has done for us, and I think he expects that his goodness to us will make us sorry for and ashamed of our sins. He commands us to think of his mercies and to fear him, and to serve him in truth with all our hearts.

Nightly, when the winds are low;
In the firelight's fading glow;
Ere upon my snowy bed
I have laid my weary head,
Angels seem to stoop and say,
"Have you loved the Lord to-day?"

Holy angels! come and be
Dwellers in my home with me!
Make me gentle, tender, kind,
Help me every hour to find
Sweetest joy in duty done,
Till, with you, my crown is won.

TWENTY-FIFTH DAY.

My son, give me thine heart. Prov. xxiii. 26.

And another came, saying, Lord, behold, here is thy pound, which I have kept laid up in a napkin. For I feared thee, because thou art an austere man; thou takest up that thou layedst not down, and reapest that thou didst not sow. Luke xix. 20–21.

For unto whomsoever much is given, of him shall be much required. Luke xii. 48.

And thou, Solomon my son, know thou the God of thy father, and serve him with a perfect heart and with a willing mind; for the Lord searcheth all hearts, and understandeth all the imaginations of the thoughts; if thou seek him, he will be found of thee; but if thou forsake him, he will cast thee off for ever. 1 Chron. xxviii. 9.

The sacrifices of God are a broken spirit; a broken and contrite heart, O God, thou wilt not despise. Ps. li. 17.

IT would be very wicked for me to think that I am unable to do what God requires

FOR CHILDREN. 89

of me! It would be like that wicked servant telling his Lord that he was an austere man, who expected to reap where he had sown no seed. I never like to read that verse; it seems so wicked for any one to talk to a kind master in that manner! *Our* Lord is not harsh or severe with any of us! He knows just what we are—for he made us. He knows just what talents we have— for he gave them to us. And because God is our maker he has a perfect right to require us to serve him. Does not God know us each by name? Does he not know our age and the amount of knowledge we have? I will be ashamed of my wicked and unkind thoughts of God—for I know that he only requires me to follow the light I have.

My soul is by nature full of sinful inclinations, yet God, my heavenly Father, commands me to be holy. By nature I do not love God, but he says to me, Give me thy heart; and oh, let me never complain or feel sorry that God wishes me to devote my life wholly to him.

It is a comfort to read that God will accept our willing hearts, and remember in mercy all our circumstances; but it is a solemn thought that to whom much is given from them much will be required. If he has given us a *little* knowledge, I suppose that he will expect us to *improve* it—because he will say that we might have understood what our duty was, if we had tried to learn his will.

In many places in the Bible God offers to renew our corrupt hearts, and to assist us by the Holy Spirit. He teaches us to pray that the love of God may be shed abroad within us—so that we may rejoice to serve him. It is wrong for me to say that I cannot give my heart to God, when all I have to do is to ask him to break my hard heart and make me love him. May I never be guilty of resisting the Holy Spirit when he strives to make my heart warm with love to Jesus! Let me be ashamed to ask how little I can do for Jesus and yet keep his precious love to me! Surely he knows who

FOR CHILDREN.

91

do all they can to please and serve him! And he sees the tears of those who weep because they can do so little.

Tender mercies on my way
  Falling softly like the dew,
Sent me freshly every day,
  I will bless THE LORD for you.

Though I have not all I would,
  Though to greater bliss I go,
Every present gift of good
  To eternal love I owe.

Source of all that comforts me,
  Well of joy for which I long,
Let the song I sing to thee
  Be an everlasting song.

TWENTY-SIXTH DAY.

There be many that say, Who will show us any good? Ps. iv. 6.

At thy right hand there are pleasures for evermore. Ps. xvi. 11.

Trust in the Lord and do good. Ps. xxxvii. 3.

Lovers of pleasure more than lovers of God. 2 Tim. iii. 4.

But they regard not the word of the Lord, neither consider the operation of his hands. Is. v. 12.

GOD has given me a desire for pleasure. He cannot wish to see my eyes full of tears, any more than my dear mother does! I'm sure that he likes to see me bright and happy, like the little birds which sing among the trees and flowers, and like the little animals that play and frolic in the sunshine!

I wonder if there was no child in the house at Bethany, where Jesus loved to go so often. If there was, I do not believe that

FOR CHILDREN.

93

he wanted it to sit perfectly still all the time. He loved children better than any one else ever loved them; and he knows how hard it is for us to play without disturbing others by our noise! I wish that I could learn to play in just the right way, so that none would think me a troublesome child!

My dear mother seems very tired of my constant asking what I shall do and how I shall find amusement and pleasure. She says I ought not to be all the time seeking my own gratification—that it is loving myself so much which makes me so restless, and that if I would try to do something for others I should find that my own happiness would increase. She says no one ever obtained happiness by only wishing for it, or even by working hard to make themselves happy. And besides, she says that sometimes the things which give us pain, bring to us *in the end* the best happiness; and that when God permits us to be sick or sends us disappointments to bear—even these sad and uncomfortable hours will do us good, and

DAILY MEDITATIONS

procure for us a pleasure in trying to be patient and contented.

My friends tell me I shall find the most of my happiness in little things; that if I am not careless and thoughtless I shall find the sweetest and most constant pleasure in God's *little gifts*. Now I will try and see if this is true. When the rain comes down from heaven, I will sit and watch it fall, and see what it does for the dusty leaves and thirsty plants. When the sun sets I will enjoy the glorious colours of the beautiful sky. I will watch the little twigs and branches, that I may welcome the first buds of spring; and when the frost bites off the golden leaves, I will try to hear the solemn lessons which they teach when the wind makes them rustle on the ground. I know that those who love to watch God's wonderful works in nature, find a great deal of happiness! But let me find my greatest pleasure in trying to imitate the blessed Saviour, who spent his life in *doing good*.

FOR CHILDREN.

Who hears the cold and driving wind,
　Play round his warm and happy home,
And thinks not with a pitying heart,
　Of those who unprotected roam?

Who rests upon his easy bed
　With blankets soft, and pillows white,
Without a loving prayer to God
　For those who dread the dreary night?

Who *knows* the sovereign reason why
　His home with every joy is blessed?
Let grateful hearts with generous love,
　Relieve the needy and distressed.

DAILY MEDITATIONS

TWENTY-SEVENTH DAY.

God is a spirit; and they that worship him must worship him in spirit and in truth. John iv. 24.

For God, who commanded the light to shine out of darkness, hath shined in our hearts, to give the light of the knowledge of the glory of God in the face of Jesus Christ. 2 Cor. iv. 6.

O Lord, thou art our Father. Is. lxiv. 8.

And thou shalt love the Lord thy God with all thine heart, and with all thy soul, and with all thy might. Deut. vi. 5.

IT is hard for me to think of God only as a spirit! He seems then like a being far away from me, and I cannot feel certain and satisfied that he loves and remembers such a poor and humble creature as I am. And if I think of his glorious character, of his perfect holiness and justice, and of his great and terrible power—then I am afraid to speak to him from out my heart so full of sin.

FOR CHILDREN.

God knew that we could not be satisfied with only the knowledge of himself as a spirit, and so he came near to us in a human form, and showed us his glory in the face of his Son Jesus Christ. As Moses covered his head with a veil, when he came down from the mountain, when God had talked with him, because the sinful people were afraid of his shining face—so God veiled his glory and spoke to us with the gentle voice of our Saviour, and walked among us in a human form. How tenderly the great God remembers our weakness and our fears!

When I hear and know that God is a Father, I feel happy in the thought that he is very near to me! When I remember that it is from his love that I receive every gift, I rejoice that he can see me every moment; I feel like stretching out my hands towards him, just as little babies hold out their arms to go to their mothers. How can we help wishing to go to a friend who shows us such love and kindness? God is the giver of all my blessings; though I am

DAILY MEDITATIONS

so young and so unworthy, he seems never to forget that I need his care and protection. How strange and wicked it would be if I did not love him best—if I did not love him even better than I do my earthly parents and friends!

Surely no one ever has been, or can be, so good to me as my heaven.y Father; and there is no one besides God whom I ought to love with all my heart, and soul, and mind, and strength. The glorious God commands me to love him supremely, because he has made my soul capable of loving that which is holy and good; and certainly when I know that *he* is the *holiest* and the *best*, I ought to love him most of all.

O Holy Spirit, change my unholy heart, that it may love that which is holy; help me to think of all God's mercies to me, and grant that I may give my whole heart to my heavenly Father, who alone is worthy of our *best* love. Amen.

FOR CHILDREN.

99

TWENTY-EIGHTH DAY.

When the Son of man shall come in his glory, and all the holy angels with him, then shall he sit upon the throne of his glory :

And before him shall be gathered all. nations; and he shall separate them one from another, as a shepherd divideth his sheep from the goats.

And he shall set the sheep on his right hand, but the goats on the left.

Then shall the King say unto them on his right hand, Come, ye blessed of my Father, inherit the kingdom prepared for you from the foundation of the world. Matt. xxv. 31–34.

For to be carnally minded is death, but to be spiritually minded is life and peace. Rom. viii. 6.

And Enoch walked with God. Gen. v. 24.

And Noah walked with God. Gen. vi. 9.

IN the beginning when God made the world he divided the light from the darkness; and in the end of the world all nations shall be gathered before him, and he shall. separate them one from another as a shepherd

DAILY MEDITATIONS

divideth his sheep from the goats. God will put each of us just where we belong, because he will know perfectly what our characters are! He will know whether we have loved to think of him, whether we have prayed to grow more and more like him, and whether we have tried to fit our spirits for his presence or not. If we have spent all our thoughts and time here upon the earth to please and gratify our bodies, then we shall see that we have lived selfish and earthly lives! But if we have loved the Lord with all our minds, if we have thought about God and remembered him, and asked him to feed our souls with the bread of life—then the Lord, who died to save us, will welcome us to sit with those who were *spiritually* minded here in this world!

Oh! what a mercy it is that God is so willing to give us the Holy Ghost! Our minds are so dark and ignorant unless he teaches us! Did not these spirits of ours come from God, who is a spirit? Certainly we must go to him for the spiritual know-

FOR CHILDREN. 101

ledge and food we need. The blessed Spirit can put into our hearts spiritual thoughts and spiritual desires, and he can make our inclinations spiritual and holy, instead of earthly and selfish. Surely when I feel the influences of the Holy Ghost in my heart, I will praise God for his mercy, and strive to keep the blessed Spirit with me, to purify and sanctify my unholy heart.

When I pray, I will ask most of all for blessings for my *soul*. I will ask God to give me more faith, that I may believe his promises and his solemn threatenings. I will ask him to open my spiritual eyes, that I may not stumble and fall into sin and danger.

My catechism teaches me that God is an infinite and invisible Being; but if we choose we can certainly learn a great deal about the character of God, by studying the things which he has made. Everything around us shows his power and his goodness, and that he is a kind Father to us! And the gift of his dear Son to suffer upon the cross for us,

DAILY MEDITATIONS

shows us more than our minds can ever understand of his infinite love. Dear Father in heaven, help me to know what it is to live a spiritual life! Teach us what it is to walk with God as Enoch did. Take my hand in thine, and lead me to thyself.

O my Saviour, crucified!
Near thy cross may I abide;
There to gaze, with steadfast eye,
On thy dying agony.

Jesus, bruised and put to shame,
Tell me all the Father's name;
God is love, I surely know,
By my Saviour's depths of woe!

In his sinless soul's distress,
I behold my guiltiness;
Oh! how vile my low estate,
Since my ransom was so great.

Dwelling on Mount Calvary,
Contrite shall my spirit be;
Rest and holiness shall find,
Fashioned like my Saviour's mind.

FOR CHILDREN.

103

TWENTY-NINTH DAY.

What! know ye not that your body is the temple of the Holy Ghost which is in you, which ye have of God, and ye are not your own?

For ye are bought with a price; therefore glorify God in your body and in your spirit, which are God's. 1 Cor. vi. 19, 20.

Let not sin therefore reign in your mortal body. Rom. vi. 12.

Our bodies washed with pure water. Heb. x. 22.

He that overcometh, the same shall be clothed in white raiment. Rev. iii. 5.

Do thyself no harm. Acts xvi. 29.

If any man defile the temple of God, him shall God destroy; for the temple of God is holy, which temple ye are. 1 Cor. iii. 17.

Mine age is departed, and is removed from me as a shepherd's tent. Is. xxxviii. 12.

MY body is only the building in which my soul lives! It is only a tent which my spirit may use while I am on my earthly journey! But though it is so inferior to my

DAILY MEDITATIONS

soul, I must take good care of it, that it may be fit for my use, and add to my happiness. How great is the goodness which God has shown to us in the formation of our bodies!

Has God told us how to treat these bodies which he created with such skill? I find in the Bible this command, Do thyself no harm—but that was what Paul said to the keeper of his prison, when he drew out his sword to *kill* himself. To be sure I never mean to kill myself! Does it not teach us that we must not harm our bodies in *any* way?

I will thank God that I am not deaf, or dumb, or crippled. I will praise him for all the pleasant things I see; for all the pleasant sounds I hear. With my lips I will sing songs of gratitude to my heavenly Father!

My body is the temple of the Holy Ghost. Oh, let me never defile it by impure acts! I pray God to make me pure and modest in all my thoughts, that I may be holy in body and spirit. O God, give me thy Holy Spirit, that sin may not reign in my body!

FOR CHILDREN. 105

In one place in the Bible it speaks about our bodies being washed with pure water; and the saints in heaven are said to be clothed in white linen garments. I think when I read these verses, and those verses in the Old Testament, where it tells of the priests bathing so often in the lavers of brass, that God even notices whether we are clean and neat in our bodies and dress! Are not whiteness and purity signs of the holiness and cleanness of our hearts? May God help me to wash my soul in the fountain of Jesus' blood, that I may be cleansed from all sin, and may my body be kept a pure and holy temple for the Lord to dwell in!

Am I strong and well? How grateful I ought to be for health; God's sweetest gifts can give us no pleasure if we are ill and in pain! Let me never do anything to injure my health!

How long shall I live in this weak yet wonderful body? God only can tell. He will take the tent down when it p^l

DAILY MEDITATIONS

him! When I reach the shore of the river of death, my soul must leave the body which gave it a home in this world. Who will watch to see me step upon the other side of Jordan? Dear Lord Jesus, send some loving angel to welcome me with smiles, as I pass through the gates of glory. I trust thy grace to save me!

There came a child with sunny hair,
  All fearless to the brink of Death's dark river,
And with a sweet confiding in the care
  Of Him who is of life the joy and Giver;
And, as upon the waves she left our sight,
We heard her say: "My Saviour makes them
    bright."

FOR CHILDREN. 107

THIRTIETH DAY.

And he taught daily in the temple. Luke xix. 43.

Remember the Sabbath day, to keep it holy. Exod. xx. 8.

But the Lord is in his holy temple; let all the earth keep silence before him. Hab. ii. 20.

For where two or three are gathered together in my name, there am I in the midst of them. Matt. xviii. 20.

Serve the Lord with gladness; come before his presence with singing. Ps. c. 2.

Enter into his gates with thanksgiving, and into his courts with praise; be thankful unto him, and bless his name. Ps. c. 4.

Go thy way forth by the footsteps of the flock. Cant. i. 8.

HOW happy those children must have been who went with their parents into the temple when Jesus taught the people! I'm sure they listened very carefully to see if he said anything which they could understand!

DAILY MEDITATIONS

Oh, what happy days those were when children could really see the Son of God, and hear his gracious words! The Bible says that he is in his holy temple now; and that when his people meet to worship him he is there to hear their prayers, and to accept their praise. It certainly is very different from seeing him as the people saw him in the old temple of the Jews! I must have more faith than the young Jewish children had if I am permitted to feel the presence of the Saviour in the house of God! And those who *believe* are promised better things than those who *see*. Christ said to Thomas, "Because thou hast seen me thou hast believed; blessed are they that have not seen, and yet have believed." I will not doubt that the Lord is in his holy temple. I will go into his presence with reverence, and offer my worship with a happy confidence that he is there to listen to my praise. Will not the Lord graciously reward my humble faith, if I go into his house *expecting* to meet him there? Is he not pleased with our faith in

FOR CHILDREN.

109

his promises? Will he not draw near to those who try to draw near to him?

I like best to kneel in my own room before God, and to read his word in my own dear Bible; but did not David go into the great congregation to join the people in their public worship? Did he not love to sing with them the glorious Psalms? O God, let not my heart be far from thee, while I honour thee with my lips.

The ministers of the Gospel speak to us in the name of the Lord; I ought to attend to what they say. How can I expect the sweet and holy benediction to rest upon my soul when I leave the house of God, if I have been inattentive and careless while there?

The Redeemer calls himself the Good Shepherd—does he not féed his flock in his sacred house on his own holy day? I cannot miss the privilege of going there with those who love him. Yes; I will try to hear and understand all that I can of the word preached; and the Sabbath shall be to me my best and happiest day!

DAILY MEDITATIONS

THIRTY-FIRST DAY.

Whosoever will come after me, let him deny himself, and take up his cross, and follow me. Mark viii. 34.

Believe on the Lord Jesus Christ, and thou shalt be saved.   Acts xvi. 31.

Remember now thy Creator in the days of thy youth.   Eccl. xii. 1.

I delight to do thy will, O my God ; yea, thy law is within my heart.   Ps. xl. 8.

O God, thou knowest my foolishness : and my sins are not hid from thee.   Ps. lxix. 5.

Jesus, which delivered us from the wrath to come.   1 Thess. i. 10.

Fight the good fight of faith, lay hold on eternal life.   1 Tim. vi. 12.

Lord, remember me when thou comest into thy kingdom.   Luke xxiii. 42.

THE followers of the Lord Jesus Christ are called Christians.   Christ the Lord of glory is their leader, their friend, and their

FOR CHILDREN.

Saviour. Am I following him—is he my leader? Do I love him—is he my friend? Do I trust in him for my soul's salvation—is he my Saviour? How happy I am if I can answer yes to these three questions!

Jesus does not tell us exactly how old we must be to be Christians—he does not say that one so young as I *cannot* be a Christian. Who are Christians? Are they those who know Christ and believe him to be our Saviour who forgives us our sins, and saves us from the wrath of God which we have deserved? I know that Jesus is the holy Son of God, and that he is a man also; that he calls himself our brother and yet is our divine Saviour. I will trust in him to save my soul.

Do Christians believe all that Jesus teaches? I will study the Scriptures, to know what Jesus says.

Are Christians soldiers of Christ? I will pray for strength to fight against every sin; I will ask the Lord to dwell in my heart and to conquer for me.

DAILY MEDITATIONS

Are Christians like Jesus, separate from sinners? I will love those who love the Lord.

Do Christians weep over their sins? I will repent of all that is wicked in my heart and ways; I will delight to do God's will, and his law shall be in my heart, and I will try to love it.

Do Christians work for Christ? I will try to do good and to set a holy example.

Do Christians belong to Christ? I will give myself to him, and ask him to remember me in his heavenly kingdom.

Are Christians all alike? Oh no; do not the beams of the same sun rear the tall pine upon the mountain top, and the pretty violet out of its bed of glossy leaves? Does not the sun bring forth the bud and flower from every seed, and ripen the various fruits of the earth? So will God's Spirit be the author of holy thoughts and desires in all our hearts, till we each become a temple where the Saviour loves to dwell. And as the sun shines upon the cold earth—so the blessed Spirit

FOR CHILDREN. 113

will warm our different hearts, that we may
each bring from our own garden the fruits of
faith and love, to the praise of him who died
to save us.

Jesus! thou art the sinner's Friend;
　As such I look to thee;
Now, in the fullness of thy love,
　O Lord! remember me.

Remember thy pure word of grace—
　Remember Calvary;　　-
Remember all thy dying groans,
　And, then, remember me.

Lord! I am guilty—I am vile,
　But thy salvation's free;
Then, in thy all-abounding grace,
　Dear Lord! remember me.

And when I close my eyes in death,
　When creature helps all flee,
Then, O my dear Redeemer God!
　I pray, remember me.

PRINTED BY

J. E. TAYLOR AND CO., LITTLE QUEEN STREET,

LINCOLN'S INN FIELDS.

BOOKS FOR THE YOUNG

PUBLISHED BY

ALEXANDER STRAHAN

[SPECIMEN OF THE ILLUSTRATIONS.]

STORIES TOLD TO A CHILD.

BY THE AUTHOR OF 'STUDIES FOR STORIES.'

With 14 Illustrations by ELTZE, HOUGHTON, and LAWSON.

32mo; gilt edges, 3s. 6d.

[SPECIMEN OF THE ILLUSTRATIONS.]

THE GOLD THREAD. A Story for the Young.
By NORMAN MACLEOD, D.D.
Illustrated by Watson, Steell, and Macwhirter.
3s. 6d. Cheaper edition, 2s. 6d.

"This is one of the prettiest, as it is one of the best children's books the language."—*Caledonian Mercury.*

[SPECIMEN OF THE ILLUSTRATIONS.]

WORDSWORTH'S POEMS FOR THE YOUNG.
Illustrated by JOHN MACWHIRTER and JOHN PETTIE.
With a Vignette by MILLAIS. 3s. 6d.

"A perfectly charming book for the young."—*Reader.*

[SPECIMEN OF THE ILLUSTRATIONS.]

THE MAGIC MIRROR:
A ROUND OF TALES FOR OLD AND YOUNG.

By WILLIAM GILBERT.

Crown 8vo, illustrated. 5s.

"The stories are well told in the best style for children, and the little woodcuts to illustrate them have the merit of showing an unhackneyed mode of treatment."—*The Times.*

[SPECIMEN OF THE ILLUSTRATIONS.]

DEALINGS WITH THE FAIRIES.
By GEORGE MACDONALD,
Author of 'David Elginbrod,' 'Alec Forbes of Howglen,' etc.
With Illustrations by ARTHUR HUGHES.
32mo, gilt edges. 2s. 6d.

[SPECIMEN OF THE ILLUSTRATIONS.]

LILLIPUT LEVEE.
POEMS OF CHILDHOOD, CHILD-FANCY, AND CHILD-LIKE MOODS.
With Twelve Illustrations by J. E. MILLAIS, G. J. PINWELL,
B. BRADLEY, and others.
New Edition, 32mo, gilt edges, 2s. 6d.

[SPECIMEN OF THE ILLUSTRATIONS.]

THE WILL O' THE WISPS ARE IN TOWN
AND OTHER NEW TALES.
By HANS CHRISTIAN ANDERSEN.
Translated by AUGUSTA PLESNER and S. R. POWERS.
With Illustrations by M. E. EDWARDS and others.
32mo, gilt edges, 2s. 6d.

[SPECIMEN OF THE ILLUSTRATIONS.]

THE WASHERWOMAN'S FOUNDLING.
By WILLIAM GILBERT,
Author of 'Dr. Austin's Guests,' 'The Magic Mirror,' etc.
With Illustrations by W. SMALL. 32mo, gilt edges, 2s. 6d.

[SPECIMEN OF THE ILLUSTRATIONS.]

EDWIN'S FAIRING.
By EDWARD MONRO, M.A.,
Author of 'Harrie and Archie,' etc.
With Illustrations by W. Jones. 32mo, gilt edges, 2s. 6d.

[SPECIMEN OF THE ILLUSTRATIONS.]

A New Edition of

ÆSOP'S FABLES.

With Illustrations by J. Wolf, T. Dalziel, Zwecker, and others.

32mo, gilt edges, 2s. 6d.

DAILY DEVOTIONS
FOR CHILDREN.

32mo.

<hr>

DAILY MEDITATIONS
FOR CHILDREN.

32mo.

<hr>

THE POSTMAN'S BAG.

A STORY-BOOK FOR BOYS AND GIRLS.

By JOHN DE LIEFDE.

New Edition, illustrated.   3*s.* 6*d.*

"We know several little children who are never weary of these little stories, and we are sure that they can learn from them nothing but what is good."—*London Review*.

"In this pretty little volume we do not get any of Mr. de Liefde's more elaborate tales; it is professedly a 'book for boys and girls,' and is made up of short stories and fables, the very things to win children's hearts."—*Patriot.*

Printed in the USA
CPSIA information can be obtained
at www.ICGtesting.com
LVHW022332050724
784742LV00003B/677